FUN FINDING OUT

ALL KINDS OF ANIMALS

Rosie McCormick   Anthony Lewis

Kingfisher

To Emily – RMC
To Kathryn – AL

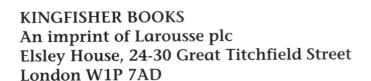

KINGFISHER BOOKS
An imprint of Larousse plc
Elsley House, 24-30 Great Titchfield Street
London W1P 7AD

First published by Kingfisher 1997
10 9 8 7 6 5 4 3 2 1

A CIP catalogue record for this book is available from the British Library.

ISBN 0 7534 0140 1

The rights of Rosie McCormick to be identified as
author of this book and Anthony Lewis to be
identified as illustrator of this book have been
asserted by them in accordance with the
Copyright, Designs and Patents
Act, 1988.

Series editor:
Sue Nicholson
Series designer:
Kathryn
Caulfield
Consultant:
Chris Catton
Printed in Singapore

Contents

What is an animal?   4

Animal homes   6

Mammals, big and small   8

Looking at birds   10

Reptiles and amphibians   12

The world of insects   14

Animals in the ocean   16

Animals in hot places   18

Animals in cold places   20

Families on the farm   22

Horses and ponies   24

Finding out about cats   26

All about dogs   28

Taking care of animals   30

Index   32

What is an animal?

The world is full of all kinds of animals.

There are frogs that hop,

snakes that slither

and birds that fly.

Because there are MILLIONS of animals in the world, scientists have arranged them into groups. Each group is different, but every animal needs oxygen to breathe and food to eat to give it energy to grow.

Mammals feed their babies on warm milk from the mother's body. We are mammals, too.

Reptiles have scaly skin. Most reptiles lay eggs but some have live babies.

Amphibians lay eggs in moist or wet places. They can live on land or in fresh water.

How many legs?

Some animals have no legs. Others have two, four, six or eight legs. And some have so many legs, they are hard to count. How many legs have these animals?

Worm

Ostrich

Tiger

Beetle

Spider

Centipede

Insects have six legs and hard, armoured bodies. Most insects lay eggs.

Birds have soft feathery wings and most can fly. All birds lay eggs.

Fish live in salty sea water or in freshwater lakes and rivers. Most fish lay eggs.

Animal homes

Animals live everywhere. They live under the ground, in tall treetops, in winding rivers and in salty seas and oceans. Their homes are often out of reach or hidden away from other animals to keep them safe.

Some wasps build nests in trees.

Ducks build nests which are hard to spot in the reeds.

Foxes live in holes called 'earths' which they usually dig themselves.

Water voles dig long burrows in banks near water.

A snail's home is a hard, round shell which it carries on its back

Nice and warm

Sometimes people build or buy homes for animals to keep them safe and warm.

Horse and stable

Dog and kennel

Hamster and cage

6

Squirrels build nests called 'dreys' in the tops of trees.

Barn owls like sheltered homes inside old buildings or trees. They hunt at night and hide during the day.

Spiders live close to their sticky, silky webs.

Building a home

Making a home can be a lot of hard work. Here's how a weaver bird builds its nest.

1

2

3

Mammals, big and small

Mammals include the teeny, tiny pygmy shrew and the ENORMOUS elephant. All mammals have hair on their bodies, and some have warm furry coats. Most mammals live on land. The bat is the only mammal that can fly.

Bat

Giraffe

Kangaroos and koalas are called marsupials. When they are born they are as small as a pea. They stay inside a special pouch on their mother's tummy until they are bigger.

The elephant is the biggest and heaviest animal living on land.

The giraffe is the tallest animal.

Elephant

Koala

Kangaroo

Gorilla

Lion

Baby pygmy shrews hold on tightly to each other's tails so that they don't get lost.

Some mammals, such as the shy, gentle gorilla, eat leaves. Plant-eaters are called herbivores.

Lions and tigers eat mostly meat. Meat-eaters are called carnivores.

Pygmy shrew

Monkey business

Monkeys and apes swing from tree to tree using their hands and feet to grasp the branches. Some use their tails, too.

Woolly monkey

Chimpanzee

Spider monkey

Orang utan

The blue whale

The largest animal of all is a mammal that lives in the ocean – the blue whale. It feeds on a kind of tiny shrimp, called krill.

A whale's tail parts are called 'flukes'.

A full-grown blue whale is so long that eight elephants could stand along its back.

Looking at birds

Birds lay eggs of many different sizes and colours. A baby bird hatches out of each egg by cracking open the shell with its beak.

Robin   Sparrow   Crow   Guillemot   Kiwi   Eagle

1 The mother bird sits on her eggs to keep them warm.

2 A tiny chick hatches from each egg.

What birds eat

Insects

Worms

Fish

Where birds live

Most birds build safe, warm nests for their eggs and chicks.

Woodpeckers live in trees.

This owl lives in a barn.

Puffins live by the sea.

3 When the baby birds hatch, their parents are busy bringing them food.

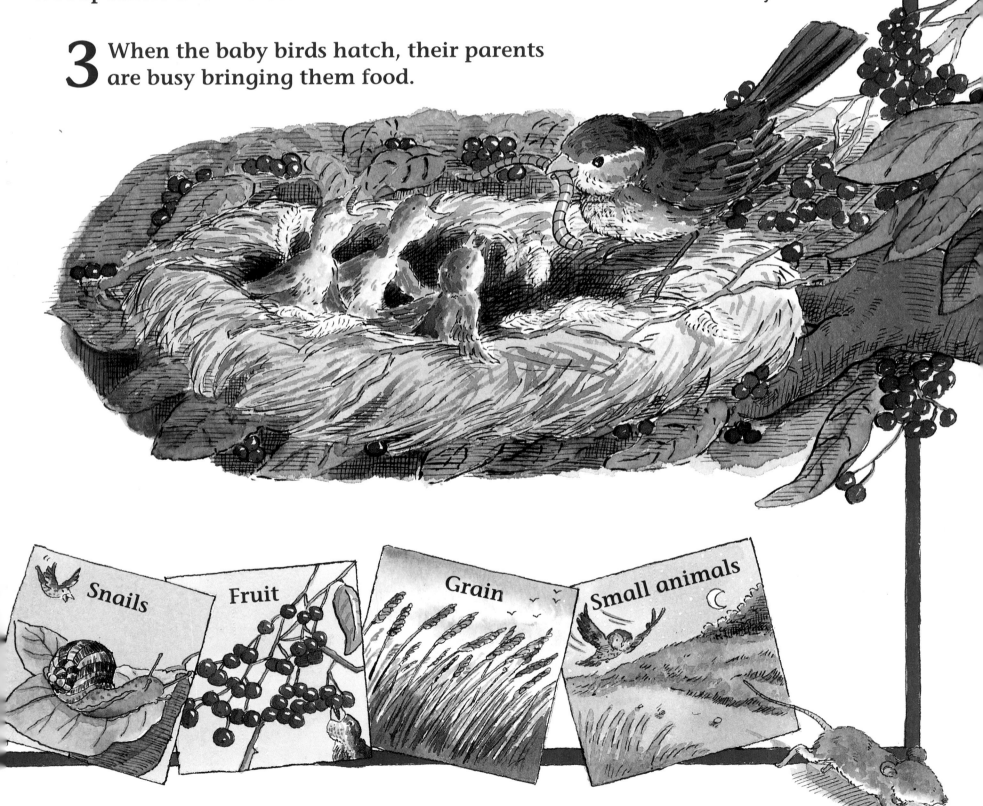

Snails

Fruit

Grain

Small animals

Lizard

Chameleons

Reptiles and amphibians

Most reptiles hatch from eggs laid on land. Lizards, snakes, turtles and crocodiles are all reptiles. So were the dinosaurs that lived long ago. Amphibians include frogs, toads, newts and salamanders.

Banded gecko

Alligator

Crocodile

Crocodiles and alligators are the biggest reptiles of all. They can grow as long as a car!

Snake surprise

...and wriggle...

Baby snakes hatch out of soft, rubbery eggs.

When a snake gets too big for its skin, it grows a new one.

Some snakes have poisonous bites.

Snakes hiss...

...and wiggle.

The world of turtles

On land, turtles move slowly because they are carrying their heavy shells. But when they swim in the salty sea, they become super speedy!

1 Green turtles lay their eggs on sandy beaches.

2 Each nest can have 200 hatchlings.

3 The tiny hatchlings crawl to the sea.

Tortoises live on land. When a tortoise feels frightened, it pulls its head and legs inside its shell.

Pond life

Toad

Amphibians begin their lives as eggs laid in fresh water. They cannot live in salty water so there are none in the sea.

1 Female frogs lay their eggs (called frogspawn) in spring.

2 After 10 days, tiny tadpoles hatch from the eggs.

3 The tadpoles become bigger and slowly turn into frogs.

Crested newt

Salamander

The world of insects

There are at least a million different kinds of insect creeping and crawling about.

Wasp

Ladybird

Small copper butterfly

Damsel fly

Bumble bee

Bluebottle fly

Brimstone butterfly

Swallowtail butterfly

Large white butterfly

Earwig

Queen laying eggs

Egg room

Pupae room

Nursery hatchery

Inside an ant's nest

14

The life of a peacock butterfly

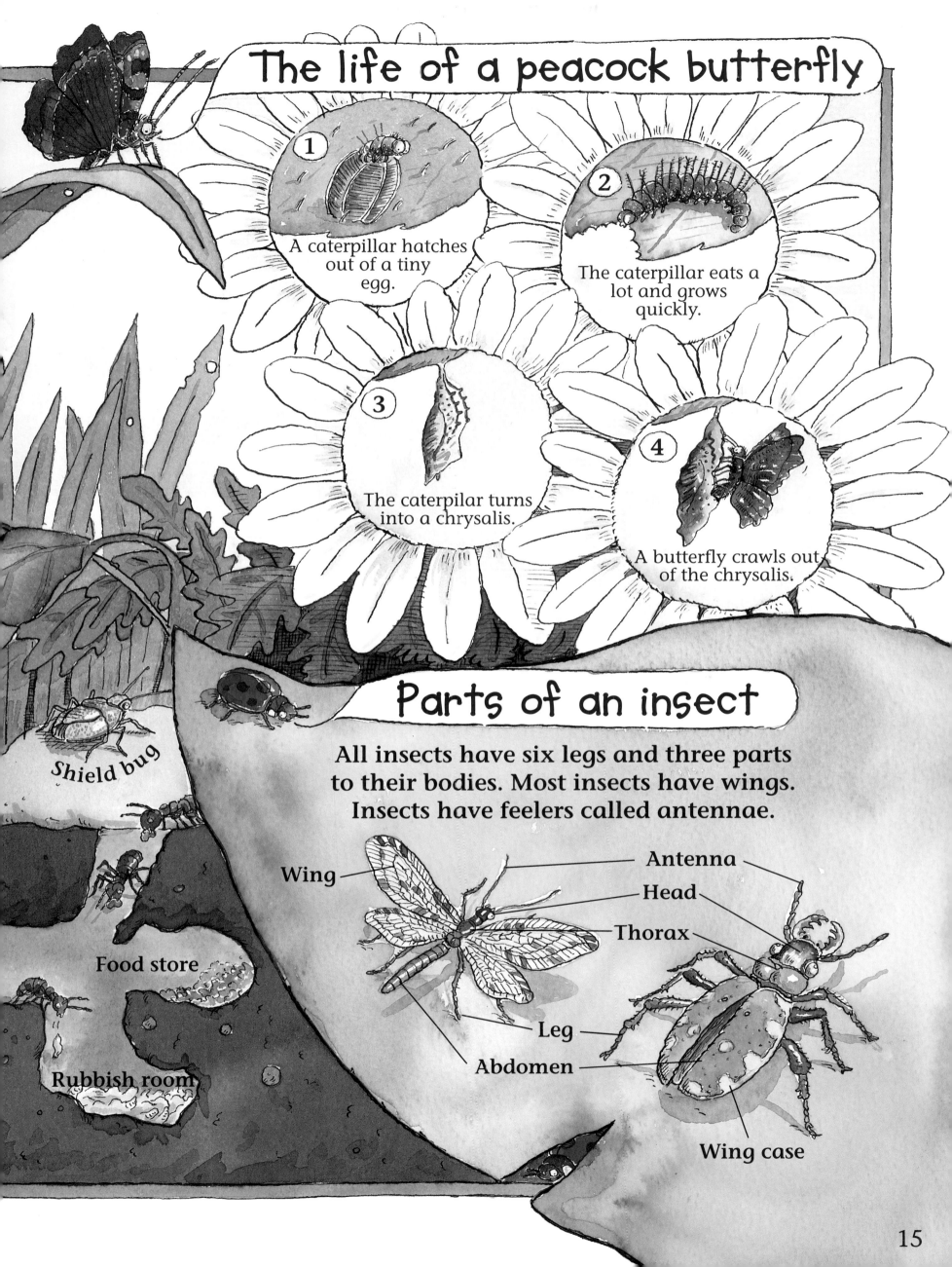

1. A caterpillar hatches out of a tiny egg.

2. The caterpillar eats a lot and grows quickly.

3. The caterpilar turns into a chrysalis.

4. A butterfly crawls out of the chrysalis.

Shield bug

Food store

Rubbish room

Parts of an insect

All insects have six legs and three parts to their bodies. Most insects have wings. Insects have feelers called antennae.

Wing

Antenna

Head

Thorax

Leg

Abdomen

Wing case

Animals in the ocean

Most of the Earth is covered with water and millions of animals live in its oceans and seas. Some live near the sparkling surface. Others live deep down in the inky darkness.

Most fish push through the water by flicking their tails from side to side. They use their fins to steer, start and stop.

Dolphin

Blue shark

Octopus

Skate

Lobster

The angler fish lives in deep water where it is dark and cold.

Jellyfish

Herring

Squid

Moray eel

Cod

Seahorse

Parts of a fish

Fish are all kinds of colours, shapes and sizes. Most fish are covered with scales. Fish don't have eyelids so their eyes are always open.

Tail

Fin

Gill slit

Eye

Scale

Mouth

17

Animals in hot places

Hot dry deserts and steamy jungle forests are home to thousands of animals. This is a South American forest. Animals live in its deep, winding rivers, on the shady ground and high up in the leafy treetops.

Toucan

Trogan

Hummingbird

Blue morpho butterfly

Can you find us?

Some forest animals are poisonous. Others have clever disguises to keep them safe. Can you find these animals?

Arrau turtle

Sloth

Tapir

Poison arrow frog

Great potoo

Sheep

Cows

Pigs

Ducks

What do these animals give us?

Cow

Sheep

Hen

Egg

Milk

Wool

Horses and ponies

Horses and ponies are strong, graceful animals. When they run, they seem to go as fast as the wind. Some horses live happily in the wild. Others live with us on farms or in stables.

Shire horses are big and slow. In the past, they were often used to pull heavy loads.

Shetland pony

Ponies are smaller than horses. They are strong and hardy.

Arab horses are lean and fit and can run very fast.

Horse relations

All of these animals are related to the horse.

African wild ass

Zebra

Indian onager

Donkey

Working horses

Some horses have to go to work each day.

This horse helps the police patrol the streets and control traffic.

This horse helps to round up cattle on the great plains in South America.

This Lipizzaner horse is a specially trained show horse.

'Points' of a horse

The parts of a horse's body are called its 'points'.

Tail

Mane

Ears

Withers

Cheek

Muzzle

Thigh

Belly

Chest

Hindleg

Shoulder

Knee

Foreleg

Fetlock

Hoof

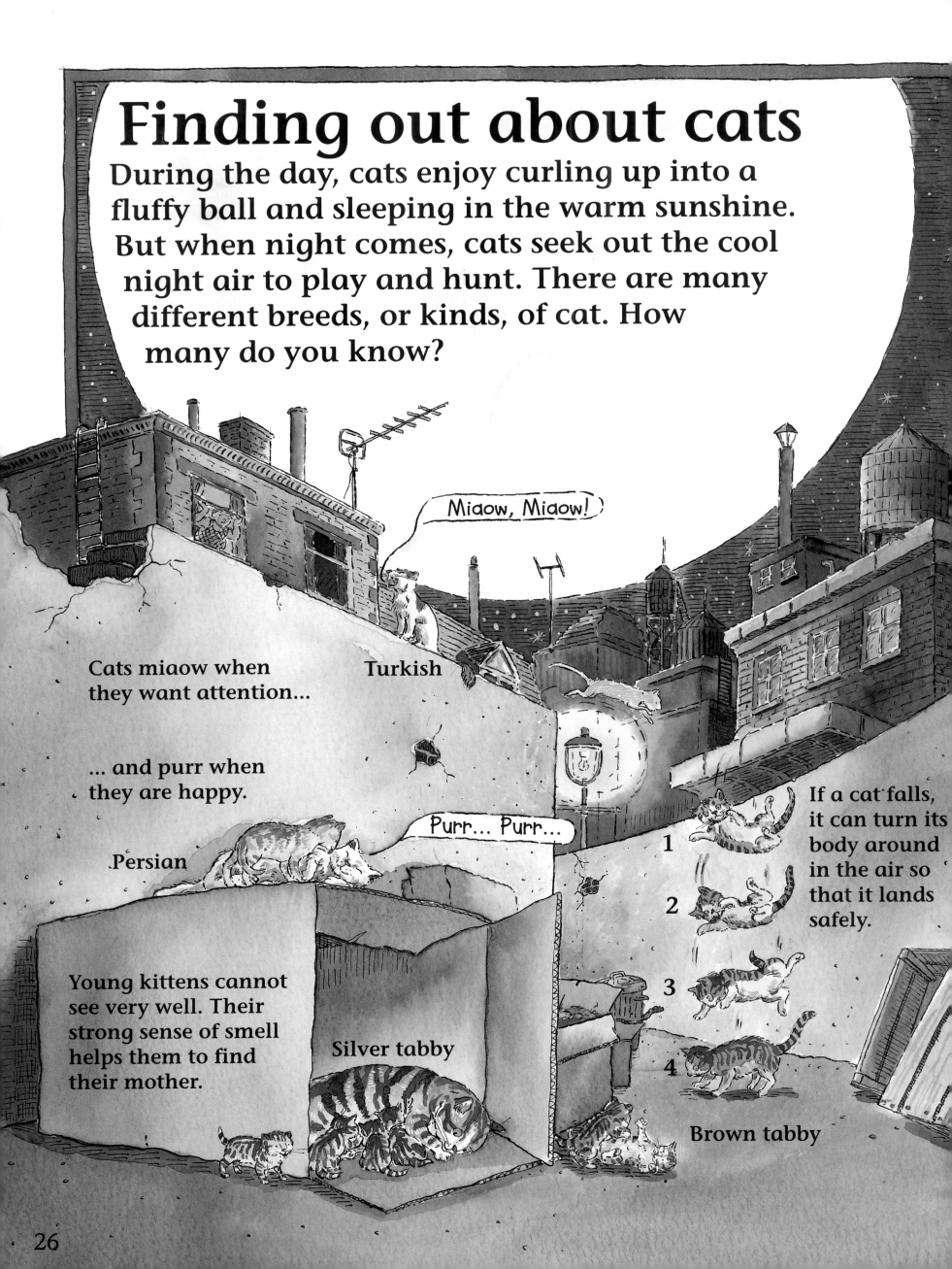

Finding out about cats

During the day, cats enjoy curling up into a fluffy ball and sleeping in the warm sunshine. But when night comes, cats seek out the cool night air to play and hunt. There are many different breeds, or kinds, of cat. How many do you know?

Miaow, Miaow!

Cats miaow when they want attention...

Turkish

... and purr when they are happy.

Purr... Purr...

If a cat falls, it can turn its body around in the air so that it lands safely.

1

2

Persian

3

Young kittens cannot see very well. Their strong sense of smell helps them to find their mother.

Silver tabby

4

Brown tabby

In the stable

Horses must be given enough food, clean water and fresh straw every day.

They should also be brushed to remove dust and mud from their coats.

The water in a tropical fish tank should be kept at a warm temperature. It should also have a water pump, to keep the water fresh.

Rabbits need roomy hutches, clean straw...

... and fresh vegetables.

Hamsters also need fresh water and food every day. Their cages should be kept clean and should include an exercise wheel so the hamsters can keep fit.

Index

A
Alligator 12
Anaconda 19
Angler fish 16
Ant 14, 19
Anteater 19
Arab horse 24
Arctic fox 21
Arctic tern 21

B
Banded gecko 12
Beetle 5
Bluebottle fly 14
Blue whale 9
Bumble bee 14
Butterfly 14

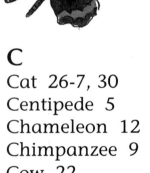

C
Cat 26-7, 30
Centipede 5
Chameleon 12
Chimpanzee 9
Cow 22
Coyote 28
Crocodile 12

D
Damsel fly 14
Dingo 28
Dog 6, 22, 28-9, 30
Dolphin 16
Donkey 24
Duck 6

E
Eagle 10
Earwig 14
Elephant 8

F
Fish 5, 10, 16-7, 31
Flying frog 19
Fox 6
Frog 4, 13, 18

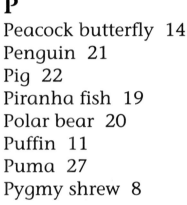

G
Gecko 12
Giraffe 8
Gorilla 8
Great potoo 18

H
Hamster 6, 31
Hen 22
Herring 17
Horse 6, 22, 24-5, 31
Hummingbird 18

J
Jackal 28
Jaguar 19
Jellyfish 17

K
Kangaroo 8
Koala 8

L
Ladybird 14
Leaf-cutter ant 19
Leopard 27
Lion 8, 27
Lizard 12
Lobster 16
Long-eared owl 7
Lynx 27

M
Macaw 19
Monkey 9
Moray eel 17

N
Newt 13

O
Octopus 16
Onager 24
Orang utan 9
Ostrich 5
Owl 7, 11, 21

P
Peacock butterfly 14
Penguin 21
Pig 22
Piranha fish 19
Polar bear 20
Puffin 11
Puma 27
Pygmy shrew 8

R
Rabbit 30, 31

S
Salamander 13
Seahorse 17
Seal 20
Shark 16
Sheep 22
Shetland pony 24
Shield bug 14
Shire horse 24
Shrew 8
Skate 16
Sloth 18

Snail 6, 10
Snake 4, 12, 19
Snowy owl 21
Sparrow 10
Spider 5, 7
Spider monkey 9 19
Squid 16
Squirrel 7

T
Tapir 18
Tiger 5, 8, 27

Toad 13
Tortoise 13
Toucan 18
Tree boa 19
Tree frog 18
Trogan 18
Turtle 13, 18

W
Walrus 20
Wasp 6, 14
Water vole 6
Weaver bird 7
Whale 9, 21
Wild ass 24
Wolf 28
Woodpecker 11
Woolly monkey 9
Worm 5, 10

Z
Zebra 24